Rocky's
Rules

Rocky's *Rules*

A PLAYBOOK FOR BECOMING
YOUR BEST IN CHALLENGING TIMES

ROCKY BOIMAN

ORANGE *frazer* PRESS
Wilmington, Ohio

Published for the author by:
Orange Frazer Press
37½ West Main St.
P.O. Box 214
Wilmington, OH 45177

For price and shipping information, call: 937.382.3196
Or visit: www.orangefrazer.com

Book and cover design by:
Kelly Schutte and Orange Frazer Press

Library of Congress Control Number: 2020910013

First Printing

DEDICATION

To my parents, who guided me
but never paved my way.

To my three sons, Beau, Bronson, and Bryce.
My greatest joy in life is being your father.

To my wife, Kelli, the love of my life. You are the
greatest supporter a man could ask for.

TABLE OF CONTENTS

PREFACE

This book is not a memoir. I do not feel my life and football career are particularly unique or special. This book is not about my accomplishments. However, I do know that my experiences playing football at the University of Notre Dame, and my eight years in the NFL taught me some profound lessons and helped shape me into the man I am today. There were highs like winning a Super Bowl with the Colts in 2006 as well as many lows, like getting cut four different times along the way. Football, particularly at the professional level, is a results-driven, unrelenting world. Because of that, it is a great proving ground to find out what you're made of.

About two years ago I started writing down my most profound experiences and what exactly it was that I gained from having lived them. Along the way, I came across a copy of a book called *12 Rules for Life* by the brilliant psychologist Jordan Peterson. It contained his twelve "rules" or guidelines for how we can live properly and flourish both as people and as a society. That inspired me to think to myself: what are my "rules" for life? After much thought and reflection on my life's experiences, especially through the lens of my NFL career, I began to compile a list of what I felt were some quintessential rules to live by that could help us become our best and live responsibly.

I think that one of the most important things we can do in life is to work every day to become the best version of ourselves. Of course, being our best is not always easy to do. The truth is, all of us need help along the way to achieve greatness. In my own case, the incredible experiences I had in college and professional football would not have been possible without the help of two wonderful parents, an untold number of talented and hardworking teammates, and some amazing coaches. The wisdom I attained—through a failure, a misstep, or an awakening—I put into these pages in hopes that you might find them helpful.

This book is simply one man's opinion on how to best equip your soul to withstand the failures, the heartaches, and the toils of life ... *and win.*

AUTHOR'S NOTE

April, 2020. As this book is being completed and
sent off to print, the country finds itself in the midst
of its biggest crisis on American soil since the Great
Depression: the COVID-19 pandemic. It has thrown
everyone's life into turmoil, disrupting our normal
routines, ravaging the nation's economy, and most
terribly, taking the lives of precious loved ones
and family members. These are challenging times
indeed. However, there is no question in my mind
that we will overcome. America and its people are
the strongest, most resilient bunch the world has
seen. As we emerge from these dark times, we are
going to need to be stronger mentally than we ever
have been. It is my hope that the lessons I talk about
in this book can serve as a small guideline to help

us pick up the pieces. We must have no excuses, and no explanations as we struggle to reemerge from the devastation and restore our economy. We must be organized to rebuild the fabric of our country. We must be strong as we face countless setbacks along the way. We must not see ourselves as victims of circumstance, knowing that everyone has been affected, some much more than others. We must not wallow in the heartache and ruin of the past, rather, we must go forward to the brighter days that lie ahead. We WILL make it.

Rocky's
Rules

ONE

PREPARE, AND ONE DAY YOUR CHANCE WILL COME

Another week, another game, and my blood was boiling. How much hard work can a person put in without seeing results? How long can one go on preparing without getting the chance to perform? This was where my head was in the fall of 2003. It was my second season with the Tennessee Titans and I was coming to grips with the reality that I was a back-up with no realistic shot at being able to crack the starting lineup. My first season had been a success. I was the Titans top special teams player and had gotten some playing time on defense as a linebacker here and there.

Going into season two, I had performed extremely well in training camp and the coaches were really taking notice. But as far as being able to be the man out there on the field, it wasn't happening. We had some really good linebackers in front of me on the depth chart, all with much more experience. I was trapped in a back-up role that didn't look like it was ending any time soon.

As I struggled with my failure to crack the Titans' lineup, I thought back to some of the lessons my dad had taught me growing up about working hard and staying prepared. My dad was the definition of hard work. He had no college degree but I was always amazed at how skilled he was. Carpentry, plumbing, masonry, electric, you name it and Mike Boiman could do it. He was meticulous and honed his craft over countless hours and years. Any work that needed to be done or thing that needed to be fixed, he was ready. He always hammered home the idea that the key to success was preparation: working on your skills, focusing on the fundamentals, and staying sharp.

Thanks to my dad, I knew the importance of preparation. So, upon entering the league as a rookie, I talked with as many coaches and players as I could. What does it take to get better at this level? What should I focus on? The answer was really the same as it had been at every level of football I had played at:

reps ("reps" being short for "repetitions"). To become better at football, or anything, you need experience and tons of it. The problem though with the NFL work week is there is so much that needs to get done that the back-ups, like me, hardly got any reps in practice. So, the question I frustratingly asked was how am I supposed to get better when I don't get any reps with our defense? Coaches and older veterans however taught me the importance of getting "mental reps." A mental rep is essentially where you watch the person playing your position and put yourself mentally in that situation. You visualize yourself making every check, every alignment, and carrying out your assignment perfectly as if you were in there live. It wasn't perfect but was the next best thing to getting a real rep and the only option there was to improve.

Expanding on this advice to get my "mental reps" I took it to the next level. I developed a routine where I would stand 25 yards behind the starting defense while they were getting their reps against the scout team offense; from that vantage point, I could get the best possible view for my mental rep. I'd diagnose the offensive formation, call out the strength side, get the other defensive players aligned, then mentally perform my responsibility as the ball was hiked. I did this routine EVERY day, for two seasons.

The mental reps certainly helped, but after a while the routine became tedious. With no payoff of actually getting in the game to show I deserved to be the starter, the mental exercises, the film watching, the hours in the gym—all of it—was starting to feel pointless. So as my second season was unfolding, I started to slack off a bit. I stopped my routine of getting my mental reps and didn't pay quite as much attention as I previously had.

My linebacker coach, Gunther Cunningham, must have noticed. He kept me after a meeting one day to talk. "You're frustrated, aren't you?" he said. I must not have been doing a good job keeping that a secret. "Look Red (his nickname for me), all I can tell you is it would be a real shame if you worked as hard as you have since you've been here only to blow it just before you got your shot. If I were you, I'd keep preparing every day as if you were the starter. Do the EXACT same thing you would do if you were the guy. Watch the same amount of tape, study the same amount of tendencies, and get your mental reps. Got it?" Hearing this from Gunther, who had been coaching football for over 30 years, really hit home to me.

So, I snapped out of my funk and was in a good mental place as Week One of the season began. I did just what Gunther said. As the season rolled on, I watched game film harder than ever. I studied the opponent's offense, and took advantage of every rep, real or mental. Four weeks into the season we were heading to Pittsburgh to play the feared and dreaded Steelers. My expectations for that game were the same as the previous four: contribute on special teams and stay mentally ready for whatever else came. However, this particular Sunday, the game played out much differently when a few plays into the first quarter, the starting linebacker ahead of me went down with injury.

"Rock, get in there, you're up!" yelled Gunther.

I trotted out onto the field to join my defense in the thick of a tough drive. I was nervous as can be, now thrust into unexpected action. The first few plays didn't go well at all. I was anxious which made me hyper and scatterbrained. I missed a couple tackles and one time didn't even line up right. "Let's GO Rock!" screamed our safety, Lance Shulters, after a long Pittsburgh gain. Here was my chance and I was blowing it.

I quickly had a little talk with myself. I remember thinking that I knew I belonged out there. I was a good player and had earned the right to be out on that field. A sense of ease came over me reflecting back on all the work I had put in. All the studying, all the film watching, and all those practices standing behind the defense getting my mental reps. As soon as that clicked in my head, my confidence was regained, and I started to play.

By the end of the game, which we won, I had tackled Steelers quarterback Tommy Maddox for a safety, racked up a bunch of tackles, and intercepted a pass, taking it back 60 yards for a touchdown. A couple days later, I was awarded with the honor of the NFL AFC Defensive Player of the Week.

Not bad for a frustrated guy who didn't expect to play!

I remember gazing out the window of the team bus as it drove away from the stadium that day. I reflected on how everything had played out that afternoon and the great performance I had. But all I could really think about was how sick I would have been had that moment come and I had blown it by not being prepared. I still think about it to this very day. What if I had gotten my chance and completely embarrassed myself because I wasn't ready? I would have never gotten another chance again.

Preparing every week as if I was the starter, even when I wasn't, had made all the difference. That's how critical preparation is. You never know when your moment is going to come.

Preparation and staying ready is critical to our professional lives. Many Americans go to work every day frustrated because they feel they deserve to be higher in the company ranks. They know there is so much more they can do for the organization; they feel it in their bones. But we can't allow frustration over our current situation to cause us to lose focus. I have been around long enough in life to be absolutely CERTAIN that a person's chance will eventually come. The manager ahead of you will be out sick one day. The salesperson ahead of you will get comfortable and slack off. The boss will want to shake things up. The player in front of you will get hurt. No matter what the circumstance, one day you will be called upon to deliver. The only question to ask yourself is: "will I be ready when my moment comes?"

Will you complain that you haven't been given a shot? Will you take your foot off the accelerator and begin to coast? Will you slack off in your preparation? Or will you focus harder than ever? Will you prepare harder than ever? Will you realize your moment to shine is just an instant away?

Prepare, and one day your chance will come.

TWO

NO EXCUSES,
NO EXPLANATIONS

Entering my third season with the Tennessee Titans, I was ecstatic. I was finally going to be the starting linebacker. I had worked so hard: years of coming in early, staying late, working out, studying film, you name it, I did it. No one worked harder. The coaches were excited for me as well, they knew my time to shine had arrived.

But like many aspects of life, it didn't go as planned. During the course of our third preseason game of the year versus the Cowboys, my left hand got twisted up during a play. Walking back to the huddle, it was throbbing bad. I tried clenching my fist but intense pain stopped that from happening right away. A team trainer led me into the bowels of the stadium to have a further look at it and sure enough, an X-ray revealed what in my head I already knew: my hand was broken.

Man, what a bummer. It's safe to say that a fully functioning hand is pretty important for a linebacker. An injury like that takes lots of time to heal and that was a luxury I didn't have with the regular season just two weeks away. The coaches had me practice very little throughout the final days leading up to our season opener to try and allow as much healing as possible to take place. As bad as it was, there was no thought in my head that I wasn't going to play in that opening game. I had scratched and clawed for two solid years to get to that point, I was prepared to do whatever I had to do. The team doctors laid the situation out for me: the only option was that I was going to have to play with my hand in a "club." That means wrapping my entire hand in a cast with no fingers or thumb exposed. Just a thick, heavy ball of fiberglass that looked like a Q-tip.

It was not an ideal situation but there was nothing else that could be done. As the week of practice began for our opener against the Dolphins in Miami, I quickly learned how tough of a time I was going to have playing with that thing. You don't realize just how much you use your hands playing linebacker until you can't use one. Everything is affected: taking on blocks, shedding blocks, running, tackling, all of it becomes abnormal.

In the team hotel the night before the game I was starting to panic. I finally got the starting job and now I had to go out there and essentially play one-handed. In our final team meeting that night the coaches could sense my frustration and tried easing my mind. "You'll be okay, Rock, you'll play just fine. Don't worry, just do the best you can and you'll be great."

All right then, let's rock-n-roll.

This is the part where I wish I could tell you that I defied the odds and went out there and had a monster game … one with a dozen tackles and a sack … or maybe even a moment where I reached that fiberglass club up into the hot Miami air and hauled in an interception and returned it for a game-winning touchdown. I really wish that was the case.

Instead I had maybe the worst game a linebacker has had in the history of football. All my fears: not being able to take on and shed blocks, missing tackles, you name it, all came true in a nightmare audition.

I didn't sleep much that night after the game. Players dread having a bad performance because we know we have to go in the next day and relive the embarrassment in film session. All through the night I cursed my fate. I dreaded the entire drive into work that morning. When I finally arrived at our team facility though, everyone was in a great mood. We had won the game which is the most important thing. As I shuffled into our linebacker meeting room, I was in better spirits, too. After all, I had done the team and the coaches a solid by gritting it out and playing through a tough injury. It will be fine, I was sure.

Then they turned the film on.

I've been on the receiving end of some brutal film sessions but nothing like that. An hour straight of misery. "Rocky, why didn't you make that play?" "Rocky, you've gotta get off that block." "Rocky, why did you do *that*?" I thought hard about holding my still broken and bandaged hand high into the air and saying *helloooo, can't you see why I didn't make that play?* After a while they didn't say anything, which was in a way, worse. There really wasn't anything to be said. The product I put out onto the field that day was awful. One thing that was NEVER uttered that entire meeting or that entire day was that they understood why I played bad and that it was okay. To them, it most definitely wasn't okay.

It was right then in that meeting room that I learned one of the most important lessons of my life: No one *really* cares why you did or did not get the job done. The only things people really care about are the results. No excuses. No explanations. Just execute and deliver. That's it.

It didn't matter that my hand was broken. The coaches at that level certainly didn't care. From that moment on I realized it more and more every day. Every excuse—*coach, the sun was in my eyes, I slipped and fell, the other guy was holding me*—none of them held any water.

But what an amazing life lesson, right? And if you're really truthful with yourself, you realize it's not just in the NFL that this unwritten rule applies, it's in all of our lives.

We think the boss will understand that we were up all night throwing up and that's why we gave a sub-par presentation to the new clients. We tell ourselves it's okay that we were late to that important meeting because there was an accident on the highway. We believe that the manager will understand that it's just a tough time of year for business and that's why we didn't meet our quota.

We think people will understand. Only they really don't. No one cares. This is especially true in high-level occupations and customer service.

The "no excuses" mentality became one of my favorite things about the NFL. Professional football is unforgiving. It doesn't care if you're young or old, healthy or hurt, paid or unpaid, black or white. Did you make the play? Period. That's the only thing that matters. No excuses, no explanations.

Years later I went on to play for the Indianapolis Colts. The first time I walked into the locker room I saw a sign painted in huge letters across the back wall that read: "No Excuses, No Explanations." Turns out that phrase was one of Colts head coach Tony Dungy's favorite foundational principles as well.

I smiled and knew I was in the right place.

The sooner we realize in life that no excuses and no explanations will do, the better off we will be. We all will make mistakes along the way, that's natural.

But if we get rid of our excuses, we'll waste less time and energy explaining ourselves and have more time to learn how to be better.

No excuses, no explanations, just get the job done.

THREE

TAKE CARE
OF THE DETAILS

Being a part of the Indianapolis Colts' 2006 Super
Bowl team was the single biggest thrill of my
professional life. But it was now April of 2007 and the
team was excited to move on and embark on a fresh
new season, one that hopefully would be as successful
as the last. It was day one of our off-season mini-
camp practices, the first chance to get back out on the
field as a team and shake the rust off.

To kick things off that morning, head coach
Tony Dungy brought the entire team into the
meeting room. Before getting into the schedule for
that day, he put a video clip up on the giant video
screen in front of the room. The clip was of our
offense's first score of the Super Bowl just a few
months back in February. With about seven minutes

to go in the first quarter, our quarterback Peyton Manning found wide receiver Reggie Wayne on a 53-yard touchdown pass.

"What happened on that play?" he asked.

There were many right answers to his question. Peyton had done a great job staying alive against the rush, stepping up in the pocket and making an off-balance throw just as he was getting hit. The offensive line had done a great job sorting out the defense's pressure. Reggie had done a good job finding open space in the Bears' defense, making the catch, and taking it into the end zone.

Coach Dungy kept going around the room asking different players why the play had worked but wasn't satisfied with any of the answers. He finally said: "Here's what happened: I talked to [Bears head coach] Lovie [Smith] after the game. The Bears were worried about Peyton being able to hear the defense's checks at the line of scrimmage. To combat that, they went into the game with a wristband and hand signal system so there would be no verbal checks. The coach on the sideline would signal in a number that would correspond to numbers on a wristband that each player on defense was wearing, telling them what defense and coverage to play."

"What happened on this play," he described, "was 10 guys on the Bears defense got the signal from the sideline telling them to play coverage '#1' listed on their wristband. The eleventh guy, the safety, didn't pay close attention, glanced down at his wristband and mistakenly played coverage '#11.' He was playing a completely different defense than the other 10 guys. Busted coverage. Reggie Wayne wide open. Touchdown Colts."

Wow. So here is the Super Bowl, the biggest game on the biggest stage. In the lead up to the game, analysts on TV and radio across the nation would talk about how critical it would be for specific players on each team to step up and make big time plays. Networks would roll out highlights of past Super Bowl's greatest performances like Joe Montana's game-winning touchdown drive to beat the Bengals in Super Bowl XXIII and David Tyree's incredible helmet catch in Super Bowl XLII to help the Giants beat the undefeated Patriots. Yet our first touchdown in the big game came because of something *so simple* as a player on the Bears defense misreading his wristband and playing the wrong coverage. It wasn't some Sports Center-worthy feat of athleticism that won us that play and led to us winning the game. It was a busted coverage caused by a small but very critical detail that was overlooked.

Coach Dungy's point was hammered home that morning in the meeting: it's not Herculean efforts that win games, it's paying attention to the little details. The teams and players that do the ordinary things better than everyone else are the ones that win games.

You might recall the closing seconds of Game One of the 2018 NBA Finals: the Cleveland Cavaliers were all tied up with the Golden State Warriors. The Cavs had the ball and put up a shot. The shot was missed but was rebounded near the rim by Cavs forward J.R. Smith with 4.7 seconds left. Instead of putting up a shot to win, he inexplicably dribbled the ball out to half court and allowed time to expire. Everyone was confused. The teams went into overtime and the Cavs lost the game and eventually the series. After the loss, the world collectively asked: "Why didn't Smith put up a last second shot in regulation? Why didn't he heave a pass to LeBron James to attempt a game-winner?" The answer came shortly after the game when cameras caught J.R. Smith mouthing the words to an exasperated LeBron James: "I thought we were ahead."

Same situation. Not a buzzer-beating shot by the opponent. Not some historic performance by the Warriors Steph Curry. Not some catastrophic breakdown in the Cavaliers defense. None of it. The big reason the Cavs missed out on an opportunity to win was because a professional basketball player didn't know what the score was.

Everyone thinks that winning takes super-human effort—that you have to do something extraordinary to be successful. This mentality is quite common. Companies think they need the top 1% of talent to succeed in the market. Coaches think they need a roster of all-stars to go deep into the playoffs. Talent certainly helps but it isn't enough. Lots of companies with talented employees go bankrupt. Many talented teams never reach the postseason. The key to success isn't talent as much as it is the result of talented people minding the small, often mundane details. Day-to-day it takes people making sure they are taking care of the routine, uncomplicated aspects of their job but *nailing* every single one of them, every single time.

It really is simple stuff, but it takes FOCUS and DISCIPLINE to not let the little things slide.

Unfortunately, focus and discipline have become harder than ever in today's world. Our minds have become conditioned to instant gratification. We aren't used to waiting for anything. The items we want get bought online and appear on our doorstep the very next morning. Countless news feeds are at the tip of our fingers, so we skim the headlines, rarely reading all the information in the article. It is now commonplace for people to listen to podcasts at 1.5 or 2 times the normal speed so they can get it over with and move on to the next thing. These days, there is always seemingly something better out there and, with a quick search, we can find it. We are so accustomed to a mentality of "get it started and get it finished quick" that it often flows over into our work. We get so consumed with completing a task that we don't take the time to assure that we grasp all the information and follow every step so the job is done right.

The other thing that makes taking care of the little details harder than ever these days is the ever-present distractions from devices and social media platforms. Most of us are on Facebook, Instagram,

Twitter, Snapchat, and Tik Tok and it sometimes feels like some people are on all of them at the same time. It's harder than ever to focus on work when the buzz of a phone call, the ping of a text message, or the jingle of a social media alert is just a moment away. The more beholden to these devices we become, the easier it is to let little details slip by us. Given how accustomed we are to instant gratification and how many distractions are out there, it has become a major challenge to focus on the details and give our best effort.

If we can find the will to focus, we would quickly realize that taking care of the small details is something that EVERYBODY can do. Paying attention to details doesn't take God-given exceptional ability or a super-high IQ. It just takes a willingness to have the discipline to not let ANYTHING slide.

If your boss gives you a project, mind every detail of the task. Take your time and do it right. Have the self-control to set the phone aside, turn the social media alerts off, and get down to work. Read instructions thoroughly. Listen to every last piece of information that your teacher, your coach, or your co-worker shares with you. Don't gloss over things.

Be wise and dedicated enough to see a project all the way through. If you do that, you'll win more because the rest of the world thinks it can't be bothered with the small stuff.

Don't be so concerned with "what's next" that you skip out on "what's NOW."

Focus. Take care of the details and go win the game.

FOUR

My first NFL training camp, in 2002, was back in the good ol' days when there were real two-a-day practices. Intense sessions, most of the time in full pads, drilling, hitting, all day every day in the heat and sweat. Strained hip flexors, hamstrings, and groins. Aching joints and bloody hands. Pure exhaustion. No fun at all, and seemingly no end in sight, as any former player will tell you. In the midst of this grueling regimen it was common to ask ourselves: *"Why would the coach put us through this type of agony? All of us are beaten up physically, this can't be good for us, it certainly doesn't FEEL good."*

If you asked during training camp, most players would tell you they hated two-a-days. However, over the course of the season, we began to understand why these intense practices were demanded of us. The grueling workouts were necessary to condition our bodies to withstand the inevitable wear and tear we would endure through a five-month grind of a season. Muscles, ligaments, and tendons need to be strained in order to become resilient. The body must be battle-hardened. Even more importantly, these torturous sessions were essential to training our MINDS to be battle-hardened. Eventually, I came to appreciate the most critical aspect of the grueling two-a-day practices: they prepared our psyche, which was about to go on a 17-week journey of ups and downs, successes and failures, before the season came to an end.

Once two-a-days were finished, there was an incredible sense of pride and accomplishment. It was a badge of honor that you were able to tolerate the physical and mental pain and THRIVE where others could not. Some players fell off along the way and could not rise to the occasion. I imagine it is very similar to the feeling that armed servicemen feel as they go through basic training and have to stomach the feeling of their body wanting to quit, but their mind not allowing it.

During my early years with the Titans, I had a trainer named Dr. Ken Leistner. He was the father of what's known as H.I.T ... High Intensity Training. During my NFL off-season, I lived in the attic of his home in Long Island, New York. Dr. Ken could flat-out destroy you in a workout that took no longer than 15 minutes. It was a regimen of insanely heavy weight for reps until complete failure and beyond. He had a perfect way of breaking you in half and just when you thought you were at the absolute maximum your body could take, he would trigger you to reach into your soul and get one more rep. It was the same routine with other trainers I had throughout my playing days like Mickey Marotti, my strength coach at Notre Dame who is now at Ohio State. The purpose of the intense workouts, just like those two-a-day practices, was to push you physically in order to expand your mental toughness. If you can go through a workout to total failure and exhaustion, if you can practice twice a day, every day, for over a month, what else can you do? What other hardships can you endure?

The opposite message seems to radiate throughout our culture. The not-so-subtle message transmitted to us daily is that we shouldn't have to experience any pain or discomfort at any particular moment. Instead we should seek a life that is stress-free, easy, and comfortable at all times. If there is something hard or uncomfortable that finds its way into our lives, we should find a way to avoid it at all costs. Leisure and ease are what we should have—no, are what we DESERVE. Every invention, every app, every new fad reinforces the idea that we shouldn't be working so hard and that we should instead avoid anything that burdens us or stresses us out.

Our homes are increasingly filled with labor-saving devices. Amazon Alexa frees you from that troublesome task of having to walk all the way across the room to turn on the light switch. Kohler now makes a "smart toilet" that comes with a heated seat and cleans and dries your hind parts all while you listen to a customized playlist through high-quality built-in speakers. There is now an online service called Task Rabbit that connects you to people who will do any imaginable chore for you—move your furniture, hang a picture, cook your family a meal, do your laundry, you name it—all for a fee of course. Think of all the free time you will have to do more online shopping, social media surfing, and YouTube video binging!

Modern society has conditioned our minds to believe we should avoid even the smallest amount of discomfort. The opioid epidemic, in my opinion, has taken over partly due to the societal notion that we should never, under any circumstance, have to tolerate even the smallest degree of pain. Take a pill instead, it's EASIER. Look where that has gotten us.

All around us, American society is saying: "Take a break, treat yourself, you deserve all the comfort, all the time." But is this ultimately good for us? Is it healthy for our minds and bodies to go through the day seeking comfort after comfort while avoiding physical or mental toil at all costs? Or, just like those two-a-day practices and workouts with Dr. Ken, is voluntarily experiencing discomfort actually *better* for us?

I feel we are better off when we frequently test ourselves to see what we're made of. How we respond in that controlled environment may help us down the line when the situation is real and the consequences vital. These small tests do so much for our self-esteem. True self-esteem comes from doing things that are hard, not by being rewarded for things that are easy.

Find opportunities daily, weekly, and monthly to endure discomfort and test your ability to cope. Do your normal gym session but make it harder than you did the week before. Take the stairs every day for a week instead of the elevator. Challenge yourself to wake up half an hour earlier than you normally do. See if you can purge your house of just one item of comfort. Try using a hand tool rather than a machine to fix a household issue. Think of something that scares you and see if you can overcome it. Find ways here and there to make life difficult on yourself. Not all the time. But making sure every move you make or task you set out to do is performed the easiest way possible is no way to live.

If you can withstand the pain of pushing your body and mind through some scheduled physical and mental discomfort, what else will you be better able to handle? What about the stress of getting fired? Do you think maybe you'll find yourself to be a little bit tougher to withstand the agony of something like that? What about the unfortunate loss of a loved one? Do you think you might find yourself to be a bit more mentally strong and able to cope with that difficult situation without becoming completely broken? If you make a habit of testing yourself—

straining your mind, body, and soul—will you gain the confidence to pursue the dream you've always had or go after that job you've always wanted? I believe you will.

In your daily life, resist seeking comfort all of the time. If you see a heavy object, lift it. For no other reason than it's there and you want to show you can. Prove it to yourself. Put yourself through things that you hate. Go out in the cold without a jacket to show you can withstand it, and also allow yourself to truly appreciate what it's like to be warm. Live frugally, so that you don't become reliant, and so you can genuinely enjoy an occasional extravagance. Push your body to its physical max, so that you may wholly enjoy rest. Endure pain, so you may truly appreciate comfort, while preparing yourself for the next hardship. Train yourself. Get comfortable being uncomfortable. Do it every day if possible because the struggle will prepare you for life's other struggles.

We MUST do this. We must prepare ourselves for the fight that is Life. In testing ourselves we LEARN about ourselves. We find out where we are strong, where we are weak, and what aspects of our minds and characters need to be fortified.

Volunteer to fight small battles in your daily life to ready your mind, body, and spirit for the real fight that lies just around the corner.

Challenge yourself. Daily.

FIVE

SEEK TO BE STRONG, NOT SAFE

One of the hardest things an NFL player has to deal
with is the mental strain that comes from the near
constant evaluation and judgment that comes with
the job. Every day there is a coach, or a reporter,
or a fan assessing your play and judging your
performance. And none of them will keep it a secret
if they disapprove. If something does momentarily
slip by a coach, it is sure to be caught by the "eye
in the sky" and replayed in the film room later that
day. When you play professional football, there is no
place to hide.

As a player, the weight of constantly being
critiqued is exhausting. Make a bad play on Sunday
that costs your team the game and fans, by the
thousands, will let you have it. You had better
become mentally tough very early in your career

or you won't last very long. Many don't and they crumble under the pressure to perform in one of the most demanding businesses in the world.

It was my experience that out on that field no one was going to save you. If you were getting beat that day, your opponent wasn't going to cut you some slack and attack somewhere else. The opposite was true. Your opponent was going to keep exploiting you until you made a play or the game was over. If you tried running from scrutiny, you weren't going to get very far. If you sat around and just prayed it would go away, wishing that people would cut you a break, well, that just wasn't going to happen. As unfair and unpleasant as that may be, the criticism wasn't disappearing any time soon. There was always going to be a fan who didn't like you, a coach who didn't think you were worth a damn, and an opponent who would stop at nothing to embarrass you.

However, if you hung in there and didn't run away from it, over time you developed a thick skin and the mental grit necessary to withstand the constant analyzation. Embracing the reality that you were going to be targeted and critiqued—and often very unfairly—was the only real choice you had.

But if you think about it, in today's world, all of us are judged and criticized to some degree, often daily. In our jobs, our boss is always evaluating our performance and trying to find someone who can do the job better and cheaper if they can. In schools, children are bullied and young adults are sometimes tormented by their peers. Through the pervasiveness of social media in our culture, we've all had our lives opened up to unfair ridicule, scorn, and prejudice by nameless, faceless people on the internet. Social media has become a ubiquitous part of our culture and trolls hiding behind a keyboard won't think twice about ripping you to shreds simply to get a meaningless chuckle out of it. Whether it's in person or over the interweb, one thing is for certain: our world is often a very cruel place.

Dealing with the ever-present judgment and hostility that's out there has become a problem for our young people. According to the Centers for Disease Control, suicide rates for Americans aged 10 to 24 rose 56% between 2007 and 2017. Teen depressions shot up 63% during that same time frame. The rise of social media, cyber bullying, and just the overall awful way we treat each other have become major factors contributing to anxiety, depression, and suicide.

Is all the judging, bullying, and scorn that is tearing people up sickening and unfair? Of course it is, that's no real question. But should we continue to scream at the top of our lungs how horrible it is and pray that one day it's all going to go away? Should we really wait around for kids to treat other kids better? Should we count on the idea that we're all going to wake up one day and every adult is going to start speaking to one another with respect? That would be nice, but it is a complete fantasy. It's never going to happen. In a world of 7.5 billion people, you're never going to get rid of all the cruelty and discrimination. Yes, you should be kind. Yes, you should speak out. Yes, you should stand up to bullying. But there is too much evil out there to try and root out every instance of it. Wishing it would all just stop is foolish.

How many of us deal with bullying and toxicity is also counterproductive. Fear of unfair criticism sometimes can lead us to react poorly to well-intentioned criticism. We need to be told when we're doing something wrong, that's how we get better. But that anxiety sometimes leads us to avoid situations altogether where we know we may be subject to assessment and we miss out on opportunities.

Instead of withdrawing from the world or overreacting to conflict and criticism, we should strengthen our minds to WITHSTAND. Rather than waiting for the day of bullying to end we must bolster our consciousness to ENDURE. We have to teach ourselves to not run from an uncomfortable situation or look for someone to save us. We need to stare our enemies and anxieties down and show them we won't be destroyed.

Right now, on college campuses across the nation, students and faculty seek to censor groups or speakers that they don't agree with or find offensive. They can't deal with thoughts or speech that is different from their own. Similarly, some schools nationally have replaced the traditional grading systems, A, B, C, D, F, with grade systems that are less harsh, more optimistic, and more focused on a student's emotions. In an effort to avoid criticism and make our kids *feel* better, we've sacrificed what should be the main focus: student improvement.

Mentally strong people don't get upset when others speak their minds and they welcome honest feedback and assessment.

I've always experienced that getting the cold, hard facts in life are the best things for growth.

That coach in the NFL meeting room would flat out tell me if I played poorly and would do it right there in front of my other teammates. While it didn't feel good, I realized that had he held his tongue, I wouldn't have made the correction needed to get better. We have to embrace the feeling of being told that we didn't get the job done. If it's something you've failed at, learn from it.

If it's a feeling that is unpleasant, be determined to cope with it. If it's someone who torments you, block them out. Don't give them the satisfaction of knowing they are getting to you. If it's someone who doubts you, prove them wrong. Don't let negative people burn you down. Instead, allow them to become fuel to your fire. The past negative experiences you've had can become the greatest things that ever happened to you if you allow them to affect you the right way.

What's true for you is equally true for your kids. Don't run around trying to soften every blow for them. Instead of giving our kids safety, give them strength. Equip them with the tenacity and fortitude to persist through tough times and be able to pave their own way. We must teach them to endure a bully's insults or a troll's defamatory tweets. We must allow our kids to fail and experience negativity without constantly running to their rescue. Parents waste so much time trying to remove every obstacle or negative influence that steps into their children's lives. The answer to coping with life's challenges and cruelties isn't a pill, or a therapist, or adult intervention. The answer is allowing LIFE, and all its cruelties, to fortify our souls and the souls of our kids so they can tolerate, withstand, and succeed. A tough, calloused spirit is one that will win.

Just as professional football players learn to move on from a bad play, smile back at an angry fan, and to survive the harsh criticism of an unsatisfied coach, all of us must learn to endure through life's inevitable pains. This is by no means easy and it's not going to feel good. But if you can hang in there, you'll be equipped with the strength and the spark needed to achieve.

Don't run from disappointment. Don't hide from someone you disagree with. Don't cower in fear of a bully.

Seek to be strong, not safe.

SIX

BE ORGANIZED

The night before training camp with the Tennessee Titans in 2002, head coach Jeff Fisher filed the whole team into the meeting room to kick things off. As the meeting was getting ready to start, I was anxious. I was a rookie, age 22, and it was my first NFL training camp. My mind was spinning, fearing the unknown. What was my first camp going to be like? What should I expect? How should I prepare myself for this grueling marathon?

My fears of the unknown were eased a few minutes into the meeting when Coach Fisher mapped out the entire schedule of training camp. All six weeks. Every detail. What time each meeting was. What time each practice started. The length of each practice was listed. Sitting in that meeting room I could tell you what time I would be eating lunch a month from then.

This struck me as odd. Why do this?

Coach Fisher then began to explain just how much needed to be done to get ourselves ready for the season. So many fundamentals needed to be practiced. So many situations needed to be rehearsed. So many offensive plays needed to be installed. So many defensive schemes needed to be repped. If you wanted to win a championship then there was absolutely not one second to waste. Organizing our days for the next month-and-a-half was the most efficient way to maximize our time and make sure we would be prepared for every moment. And once fall camp was over, the strict regimen wasn't going to stop; it would continue like that throughout the season.

The level of organization and efficiency in the NFL work week is something to behold. You might think that there is so much time in a week to prepare for an opponent but there isn't. So many factors to consider: What areas did we fall short on the game before? How many injuries were we dealing with and which backups needed to be ready to play? What were the strengths and weaknesses of the upcoming opponent? What was the weather going to be? With all those factors and more, in one of the most highly competitive fields in the world, strict time management of all the variables wasn't really a choice.

If you ever get an opportunity, go check out an NFL training camp practice. They are usually open to the public for anyone to attend. Pay close attention to how the practice is structured. The entire session is mapped out in five-minute increments that have all been discussed at length by the coaches in their staff meetings earlier that day. Every coach gets a practice schedule, a sheet with every period of that practice typed out as a reminder of how every minute of that day will go.

The day starts with meetings: a kicking game meeting is usually first, then a full team meeting, followed by position breakdowns. Once on the field, the horn blows and practice begins with a ten-minute team stretch. From there, a "walk-through" period usually comes next where certain plays that are deemed critical for the upcoming game are simulated at a slower speed before the players see

Fall Camp

Practice	WEDNESDAY	Schedule 8:00 - 8:15 - Kicking Meet (ALL)	9:25 - Specialist
Date	8/1/20	8:20 - 8:50 - Meet (Separate)	9:30 - Practice
Field	#2	9:00 - On Field	
Attire	PADS	9:05 - Activation	
Opponent	FALL CAMP #5	9:15 - Walk Thru	

P	DEFENSIVE LINE	LINEBACKERS	SECONDARY	P
PRE	Activation			PRE
RT	Run Thru			RT
ST	Long Arm Teach	Punt		ST
STR	Flex			STR
Diff	1' v 1s			Diff
1	Movement / Drills / Tec	Punt		1
2	Block Destruction	Stun / Stanley / 3-Drop	Footwork Transitions	2
3	Tackling Drill / Hip Flips	Tackle / Stalk	Tackle / Stalk	3
4	Key Work	Theme 7 on 7 (DEF)		4
5	Inside		1 v 1	5
6				6
7	Blitz Review w/LB	Blitz on Barrels w/DL	Position Specific	7
8	Team Blitz		1-1 (4), 2-2 (4)	8
9	Pass Rush vs OL	7 on 7 (Tackle)		9
10				10
11	Games Review Tec / Empty Check	Punt Block		11
12	Team O v D - Straight		1-2 (4), 2-1 (4), 3-3(4)	12
13				13
14	Play It			14
15				15
16	-35		1-1 (8), 2-2 (8), 3-3 (8)	16
17	50		1-1 (6), 2-2 (6), 3-3 (6)	17
18	35		1-1 (6), 2-2 (6)	18
19	15		1-1 (5), 2-2 (5)	19

ACTIVATION	
LJ	Sled / Dive / Review
GM	Chutes / Footwork / Keys
AW	Chutes / Footwork / Keys
JH	Quinn / Corners - Press Pro / Catch Tec
MB	Quinn / Corners - Press Pro / Catch Tec

Here is a sample of a typical practice schedule. Notice at the top of the chart how every minute of the morning is accounted for.

them later in practice at full speed. The coaches of each position group instruct their guys on the particulars of that play and the details of what exactly the player should be aware of. Fast, fast, fast, no time to waste. The defensive line coach tells his guys how the offensive line may try to block them. The linebacker coach may teach his guys what keys to read to be able to diagnose the play. The secondary coach may alert his guys on how a certain width or split by a wide receiver may tip them off that a specific play is coming. The horn blows again and the players break down into their position groups to work on fundamentals specific to their jobs. The position coach has preplanned what drills he intends to do and has scheduled the exact number of bags, tackling dummies, footballs, and other supplies that the equipment managers must have in a specific location ready to go. This framework continues through a variety of different periods: a pass-only drill called 7-on-7, special teams periods, full team periods, goal line, situational periods, two-minute drills, and more.

The entire practice is discussed and planned out so not one second is wasted. In the NFL, being organized wasn't "a" way to do things, it was the

ONLY way. The Eighth Deadly Sin on an NFL practice field was wasting time.

But it's not just in the NFL that proper time management is imperative. For most every single one of us, our lives are busy, packed with duties, responsibilities, and places to be. Between work, kids, soccer practices, family responsibilities, and more, there really isn't much time for any of us to waste. What really kills our productivity though is the innumerable amount of distractions that are all around us and so easy to access. When given even a brief moment of respite, we access our social media feeds and scroll endlessly or pull up YouTube and go down the rabbit hole of procrastination. Focusing, even when we have a lot to accomplish, is tough.

That's why being organized and having a schedule is so critical. Organization gives structure to your day. It's hard to start any task when things are in chaos. A messy desk, a cluttered workspace, and a chaotic environment all drain any eagerness one may have to get something done. However, when you start your day organized, you have a base, a solid place to start. Then once you've started, organization allows you to stay on task until completion.

The biggest advantage of having your life organized and adhering to a schedule is that it allows every action you take to have a *purpose*. Life is so turbulent with all of us interacting with a hundred responsibilities and distractions a day that we must find a way to cut through the clutter and make sure our behavior has purpose so we can accomplish the goals we've set for ourselves.

As mentioned before, in-season, an NFL player's days, weeks, and months are all mapped out by a strict schedule. What time each meeting starts, when you eat lunch, what time the bus heads over to the stadium on game day, what time the pregame warm-ups start. However, when a season ends or a player retires, all of a sudden that schedule—that structure—is gone in an instant. That's why incidents of players getting in trouble are so much higher in the off-season and why so many former players find themselves aimless upon retirement. They don't have that framework and organization they need to have a productive day and work towards their next goal. The same is true for all of us: lack of structure allows our time to be spent without meaning.

Unclutter your life. Tidy up the messes around you. Have a clean slate to begin your day. You'll feel so much better. You'll find yourself better able to manage distractions and focus on your goals. Make yourself a schedule the night before or the morning your day begins. Have a plan.

Be organized.

SEVEN

DO *YOUR* JOB,
NOT SOMEONE ELSE'S

During my rookie year with the Titans, we were playing the New York Giants at their home field in the Meadowlands. The Giants offense had driven the ball down the field and they were now inside the five-yard line. Our defensive coordinator, Jim Schwartz, sent our goal-line defense out onto the field. I was the outside linebacker on the right side aligned on the line of scrimmage just outside the tight end. In that situation, believe it or not, we were expecting the Giants might run a pass play. We called a "zone" defense where my responsibility was to drop to the "hook," which was the area around the hashmarks, and cover any receiver who came into that zone. I *knew* this. However right before the play I started to over-think things. I looked directly across the line of scrimmage and there stood the Giants stud tight end, Jeremy Shockey. I was determined to not let him catch a pass for a touchdown. I was going to be the hero of the day and break up the throw or grab the pass for an interception. So as the ball was snapped and Shockey started his pass route, I proceeded to cover him man-to-man as he crossed over the shallow middle to the opposite side, thus vacating my zone. Sure enough, the other tight end who was aligned on the opposite side of the formation, ran his route, crossing over to where I was supposed to be standing. He then proceeded to make the easiest touchdown catch in the history of football.

Jogging off the field after the score, I wasn't even halfway to the sideline and I could already hear it. "Rocky! WHAT THE HELL WERE YOU DOING?" screamed my defensive coordinator. I started to explain that I was certain that they were going to go to the other tight end and I didn't want him to catch the ball. And that's when he said it: "Rocky! Do YOUR job! Don't try and do the other guy's!" There were of course a few (hundred) expletives thrown in there but the point was made and it has always stuck with me. "Do your job" conveys the idea that you have to take care of your responsibilities, while also emphasizing the importance of focusing on doing YOUR job and not somebody else's.

I made the mistake that afternoon in New York because I wanted to be the hero. The desire for glory caused me to venture outside my lane. I had also done it because I didn't have confidence that the linebacker on the other side was going to cover the crossing route to his side. That was foolish. He was a professional and knew what he was doing.

Whole systems break down when we try to do someone else's job. On a Sunday, watch any football team that is getting steamrolled. Nine times out of ten it's exacerbated by players playing outside the structure of the offense or defense and trying to perform other guys' jobs instead of focusing on their own. You'll see a linebacker playing both his gap and the defensive end's gap. You'll see an offensive guard who tries to block both his man and the offensive tackle's man. Most of the time when you try to play two gaps or block two guys, you end up doing neither.

It is so common these days for people, on social media and otherwise, to lambast others about how wrong they are and try to tell them how they should do their job. Often times, if these folks would take a look at their own situation and their own job performance, they would find severe flaws. Resist the temptation to do this. Don't try to clean up someone else's house when yours is a train wreck. Instead, focus on your role alone, and ways that you yourself can get better.

Every day, organizations and companies across the world build teams to solve problems or improve the organization's success. A good leader knows that not one person is an expert in all areas. So, responsibility is delegated in a way where every member is allowed to focus on their specific area of expertise. When every individual can focus on their lone responsibility, the collective parts come together and the team can achieve its goal.

Teams run into trouble when one member tries to be Superman and solve every problem on their own. It's the house framer who tells the mason how to better lay the brick. It's the salesman who wanders outside of his area because he thinks he can get more clients. It's the mother who critiques the other kids all the while her child is a monster.

It's the linebacker who tries to be a hero and doesn't cover his zone.

Often when people wander beyond their role, their intentions are good. They want to win. They want nothing more than the company or group to succeed. But when that one person gets outside their area of responsibility, it's only natural that the success of the role they were given suffers. The other thing that happens is the person whose job you're infringing upon will start to take offense. They'll begin to wonder if you think they are inferior and can't hold up their end. Then infighting and finger pointing ensue and the cause is absolutely hopeless.

Every successful team I've been on is one where everyone knew their role ... no matter how big or how small ... and they executed that role to the fullest without ever getting out of their lane and into someone else's.

There will be times when someone won't meet expectations. But the minute you try to do double-duty, you're only compounding the problem. Eventually the weak link will be identified, and that person will be replaced. Don't augment the team's deficiencies by becoming unfocused on your role.

Fulfill each and every requirement of your position to the absolute fullest, no matter how insignificant your role may seem, and resist the temptation to try and do too much. Your spouse or partner in life is depending on you to be honorable and take care of them. Nothing more, nothing less. Your kids are relying on you to protect them and give them guidance. Your coworkers are trusting you to fulfill your responsibilities and help the team win. Make an impact and make sure it's in your domain.

Do YOUR job, to the fullest, and not someone else's.

EIGHT

DON'T EVER
BECOME A VICTIM

After my sixth NFL season, and second with the Colts, I was a free agent again. That off-season was particularly hard because I had to have shoulder surgery from an injury that happened in the middle of the previous year. My shoulder surgery scared off many teams so free agency lasted longer than it should have. The injury also hurt my financial potential. But I wound up signing with the Philadelphia Eagles and was excited to make my mark in the City of Brotherly Love.

Now in Philadelphia, I was rehabbing my shoulder, working out, and getting ready for the season. Eventually, April and May rolled around and we once again began our on-field mini-camp practices. This was an extremely frustrating time for me. Because my shoulder surgery had been only a few months prior, I wasn't able to participate in on-field work. Had I been on the Eagles the season before and had experience in that defensive scheme, it might not have been that big of a deal. But now I was having to learn a completely new system from what I had known and was comfortable with my previous six seasons. Different terminology, different responsibilities, different adjustments. I got my mental reps in and did the best I could from the sideline. However, there was no getting around it, when training camp was to start in a few months, I was going to be playing catch up.

Training camp started and sure enough, because I had missed so many valuable reps that off-season, I was behind big time. I was out there *thinking* instead of reacting and playing the way I was used to. The entire six weeks of that camp was a slog. It was frustrating but I made it through and was excited for my seventh season to begin.

On the Sunday after the last preseason game, the roster was cut down to the league maximum 53 players and I made the team. The next day, Monday, we would begin preparation for our first game. Having that afternoon and evening off before the start of Week One, I ventured out alone to my favorite Philadelphia diner to have some victory chicken wings and think about my upcoming season as an Eagle. Mid-meal, my phone rang. I didn't recognize the number but it was a 215 (Philadelphia) area code. Then my heart sank as I realized who was most likely on the other end. Sure enough, it was Eagles General Manager Howie Roseman. He proceeded to tell me that I was being released and he, of course, was very, very sorry.

Devastation. Here I was, literally getting ready for the start of Week One, and an instant later, a gut-punch and the reality that I was suddenly unemployed.

I had been released before, by the Cowboys in 2006, so I had experienced it in the past. But this situation was a thousand times worse because they had released me so late on that Sunday. Other teams had already grabbed recently released players off the waiver wire and solidified their rosters. Over the next 24 hours I spoke with my agent a hundred times and waited for the phone to ring. But it was to no avail. I was in a very, very bad spot.

Man, was I bitter. How could they do that to me? I was a veteran player who had six years of good performances on my resume. I had struggled

through the shoulder recovery, labored greatly
to learn a new defensive scheme, and shown
toughness all along the way.

About this time, I started to feel sorry for myself.
A severe case of self-victimization set in. In my head
at the time, EVERYONE deserved blame. It was the
Eagles fault for not recognizing the good player that
I was. It was the GM's fault for releasing me so late
where I couldn't be picked up by another team. It
was the coaches' fault for not believing in me. It was
my agent's fault for advising me to play for such a
crummy organization. It was God's fault for putting
me in that wretched situation. No one was blameless.

Except for me, of course. Minus making a few more
plays, I had done everything right.

And I really felt like I had. During the following
hours, days, and weeks, I rehashed every move
and every decision I had made from the end of the
previous season to the beginning of this one. I had
trained harder than ever. I studied the new defense
more intensely than I had ever studied. I met with
the coaches. I took care of my body. I ate, slept, and
breathed football. It was hard to recall one decision

I had made that wasn't about putting myself in a position to be the best player I possibly could. Why the hell was this happening then?

I became very resentful. I had battled hard and largely succeed through six years of my NFL career. I had toughed it out through injuries, had dealt with setbacks, endured demotions, you name it. I was a relentless worker. Now here I was, through no fault of my own, royally screwed over.

It was awful. In those initial days after the release, my desire to pick myself off the mat was nonexistent. It was pretty cozy lying on the ground, blaming the world for my misfortunes. It actually began to feel *good* to be a victim. I was showered with sympathy from my family and friends. There was no shortage of people who felt for me and my situation. And all that compassion felt great.

At that moment, the sulking felt good. But what about the long term? How was feeling bad about my situation helping me get up and move onward? How was being a victim empowering me to stand up and press on?

When you allow yourself to become a victim of circumstance, you destroy your ambition and drain yourself of the lifeblood needed to overcome adversity. Oftentimes, there is real truth to your view of a bad situation and you were, in fact, treated unfairly. Okay, so what next?

For the good of your soul and for the sake of reaching your highest potential, you must ACCEPT the reality of your situation, no matter how unjust it feels. Then once you do that, turn the page quickly and move forward. Standing in place and complaining isn't going to change a thing. Instead, use whatever unjust grievance that has befallen you as MOTIVATION to triumph. Use it as fuel to elevate you to heights you never previously imagined.

One day I just decided I had had enough of all this. It finally clicked that playing the blame game wasn't helping me advance one iota. I accepted my situation and vowed to prove all the doubters wrong. A few agonizing weeks later, I was picked up by the Kansas City Chiefs and went on to be a starting linebacker the last half of that season. Looking back, it was probably my best season as a player. I had removed myself from the world of victimization and self-pity just in time to go on and make something positive happen. And don't think I didn't use the chip on my shoulder from getting cut as ammunition for my comeback.

Life isn't fair. And it has never been more popular to profess to the world how bad you got it. How the world is against you. How persecuted and mistreated you are. How your current situation is unjust. We love to go on social media and scream how the coach is at fault, our parents are to blame, society is oppressing us, and God is doing us wrong.

And guess what? All of those things and more may be true!

And you'll have no shortage of people ready to commiserate with you and wail about how somehow society has wrongly allowed you to fail. However, the best thing for you as a person is to quit wasting time crying about how unfair your situation is and start getting to work overcoming it.

To become the most successful version of yourself, NEVER, EVER fall into the trap of labeling yourself as a victim.

NINE

BE FLEXIBLE,
NOT RIGID

I recall a November home game in my second season with the Titans against our division rivals, the Jaguars. The entire week of practice leading up to that game, our defense prepared for the Jags' offense to spread the field and give us a heavy dose of their passing attack. Expecting that, we installed an array of defenses with multiple defensive backs to get smaller, faster bodies on the field who were great in pass coverage. We were ready. Except when the game started, the Jaguars had a different plan.

The Jags came out in every "heavy" formation imaginable. Multiple tight ends, fullbacks, and running backs, rarely having more than one wide receiver on the field. Their game plan that afternoon wasn't to stretch the field and throw the ball all over the place, it was to pack us into a phone booth and pound us into submission. Early on, they had us on our heels.

We could have just stuck with the game plan we had practiced all week. We had spent hours and hours practicing our multiple defensive back approach, and little on run-stopping schemes that got more linebackers and defensive linemen on the field.

Of course, sticking with our game plan simply because it was what we had practiced all week would have been foolish. Instead, we adapted on the fly. Literally on the sideline between series, our coaches were drawing up alternate defenses and different personnel groups with more linebackers and defensive linemen, finding ways to get bigger bodies on the field that could take a pounding. We installed alignments and schemes that we had not practiced in weeks to counter what the Jags were doing to us that day. Changing our mindset and strategy helped us win the game.

To me, this is what separates average coaches from great coaches and average teams from great teams. The great coaches and teams don't become prisoners to what they had previously decided. They don't become frozen with fear when something unanticipated happens and just go with what they are comfortable with. When they learn new information, they don't remain rigid or stuck in a predetermined mindset. Instead, they adapt to the nuances and trudge forward.

Being inflexible can hold us back in our everyday life as well. Often these days we make up our minds about someone or something and are unable to adapt our thinking, even when new information is learned. We've determined that this coach is terrible, that politician is evil, this person doesn't know what he's doing, and we're not going to change our minds whatsoever. We remain rigid. All of us evolve throughout our lives, some more than others. As the years go by and we have new experiences, shouldn't we at least be open to the possibility of changing our assessment of things?

For much of my life, I thought of heroin users as nothing more than criminals, getting their fixes in dilapidated buildings and underneath overpasses. I now know that the heroin epidemic is something that affects millions of people from every walk of life. Rich people, poor people, public school kids, private school kids, you name it. Heroin and opioid addiction do not discriminate.

In the case of heroin, the reality of the situation changed. I experienced new information, and my image of what a heroin user looks like changed as well. A user might look like you or me. New facts open up the possibility of new ways of thinking.

I was taught growing up that you MUST have a college degree to make it in life. Having lived a few years, I now talk to friends and others who are so crippled with college debt that they can't afford to buy a house or raise a family. Many wished they had listened to their gut and instead gone into a trade that they enjoyed, holding less debt and working in a field the country desperately needs. It is now clear that you don't need a degree to have success. As times have changed, so has my thinking.

I used to think breakfast was essential to good health. Research now suggests this may not be the case. I used to think the U.S. should eliminate all tariffs. But the fact that we now lack control of essential industries that are vital to our national defense and our economy make me believe tariffs might be helpful in some cases. I used to think parenting was an easy job until I had three kids! These are just a few examples of instances where I've changed my stance on things simply because

I was open to new information and allowed my experiences to adapt my line of thinking.

It is also commonplace to dismiss people entirely based on just one or two things we don't see eye-to-eye on. It is possible to agree with someone on some issues and disagree with them on others. For instance, we can agree with someone's view on changes that need to be made in our nation's education system, but not agree with their views on fixing the world's climate. We can dislike a political leader but give them credit when they do something good. Being open to new information means being open to the ideas of people you ordinarily disagree with. It means listening. When we do that, we might come to view a situation—and a person—differently than before.

Keeping an open mind about people and situations is much easier said than done. Human beings are very tribal these days. We often get caught up in group-think because it's easier and more comfortable to just go along with our crowd. Political parties force us into camps where we can't agree with anything an "opponent" says or does even if we actually see it as reasonable! Managers can get so stuck doing business the same way they've always done that they can't see an industry change until it's too late. Ask the folks at Kodak, who used to dominate the film industry, or the people who used to run Blockbuster about that. The lesson extends to our homes too. Running our households a certain way simply because "that's how our parents did things" may not be the best strategy either as times and circumstances have changed.

Life has nuance to it. It can actually be a very exciting thing.

You should have a foundation. You should have the strong principles that you live by. You certainly don't want to be so feeble that you waffle back and forth at every turn. Being open to new information doesn't mean completely changing your mind every five minutes or abandoning your core values. But when you see something differently than you had before, don't ignore it.

Ask any football fan to list the qualities they want in their favorite team's coach and I am certain that at the top of that list they will tell you they want a coach who is able to ADAPT as the game is being played. A coach who can make adjustments between series. Someone who can tweak the game plan. Someone who can come out in the second half with a change in strategy after they have digested all the information. Be like that coach in YOUR life.

Be flexible, not rigid.

TEN

FINISH WHAT YOU START

"Even hope may seem but futile,
When troubles you're beset,
But remember you are facing
Just what other men have met.
You may fail, but fall still fighting;
Don't give up, whate'er you do;
Eyes front, head high to the finish.
See it through!"

—Edgar Albert Guest

While I personally had one of the best seasons of my career as a linebacker with the Chiefs in 2008, as a team we had a terrible season and ended up going 2-14. After the season, the club's General Manager Karl Peterson and their head coach—the great Herm

Edwards—were both fired. That meant a regime change and I soon learned that the new staff didn't have me in the plans for 2009. Once again, I was a free agent without a team.

I remained unsigned through the start of training camp that year. A couple weeks into camp, my old team the Titans, signed me. I had a really good camp but nevertheless, the last day of training camp came and I got cut again. That's the third time in my career if you're counting. I didn't know it yet but I was beginning a new and challenging stage of my NFL career. The season started, I remained unsigned, and this time it looked like it might last a while. A week turned into a month. A month turned into two months. I still kept up with my training. Five days a week, resting on Saturday and Sunday hoping a team would call that Monday to invite me in to work out for them. Every week, the same scenario, every week the same disappointment.

Football is such a wonderful game and I had loved it since I started playing at age seven. But I was now creeping up on age 30 and the handwriting was on the wall. My playing days were coming to an end, if they weren't completely over already. It was the first time in my adult life that I was forced to start thinking about what was next. Realizing it might be over scared me to death. What did I want to do with the rest of my life? I began to think about that, but there was just something inside me that wasn't quite ready to turn the page.

I had always envisioned my last day playing football would be walking off the field with my head held high. I think every player dreams of going out on their own terms, but the reality is most are forced out. The game usually says goodbye to you before you say goodbye to it. It was right in the midst of all this uncertainty and reflection that I made a vow: I was going to see the process through. The season may very likely come to an end without me getting a call from a team but I was going to control what I could and that was staying ready until the end. My dad and every coach I had throughout my life preached that you should finish what you start. Leave nothing half-completed or unresolved.

So I went back to work. As hard as I ever had. This time it really wasn't easy. You find out how much you really love football when it's late October, the leaves are changing and there is a chill in the air, and you're on some random high school field all by yourself running sprints and practicing your linebacker techniques, preparing for something that is beyond likely to happen.

October stretched into November. Along the way I was invited in to work out and audition for two teams, the Texans and the Browns, yet both to no avail. Most of the other unsigned veteran free agents who were out there had shut it down by then. Time was running out. If December 31st, the end of that season, had come and gone without getting signed I would at least be able to live with myself that I went hard until the very end. A call probably wasn't going to come but I was determined to go down swinging.

And then the phone rang. Mid-November I got a call from the Pittsburgh Steelers who invited me in for a workout. They needed help with their special teams coverage units that had been giving up a lot of big returns throughout the season. Wow. The unthinkable had happened. I was signed one week before Thanksgiving and I played in every game through the end of the season. I can't even tell you that I played that great, but it remains one of my proudest accomplishments in life. I stayed ready and saw it through to the end.

While making it to the professional ranks in football is tough, it's nothing like the grueling process to become a Navy SEAL—one of the hardest, most tortuous trials on the planet. The instructors put the hopeful candidates through a hell unlike any other. Swimming, drilling, exercising, most of the time completely soaked and with little to no sleep. If the training regimen ever becomes too much for someone to handle, there is a bell positioned near the instructor that can save them. Walk over and ring that bell and all the pain goes away. No more drilling, no more swimming, no more agony. You can go get warm and rest your tired muscles and exhausted mind. Except when you ring that bell, it's all over. You can't go back. You'll never get another chance to become a Navy SEAL. And once you ring it, most will tell you that it's something that is hard to live with for the rest of their lives.

Most of us will never go through the level of physical and mental anguish that a Navy SEAL endures. But whether you're a salesman, a construction worker, an owner of a company, a TV personality, a football player, or anything in between, all of us will be in a position one day where we will have to decide if we are going to throw in the towel and quit or keep grinding until the end.

I often think about what would have happened during that 2009 season had I shut it down and stopped my training. What would I have done when that phone call came from my agent that the Steelers wanted me to work out for them? Would I have just declined and said I couldn't do it? Would I have showed up for the workout, embarrassed myself, and made the final chapter of my playing career be one where respected NFL coaches watched me flop around on that field out of shape? One thing is for certain, I would have regretted it the rest of my life.

All of us will go through challenging times in our lives and our careers. But I truly believe that we should fight, scratch, and claw all the way to the finish line, and go down swinging if we have to. It's natural to want the agony to end and just move on, especially when the situation looks hopeless. But do whatever it takes to see it through. When you do, often you'll find yourself standing in the end. Do it for your pride. Do it for your family. Do it for your team. Do it for your soul. Fight until the end and have no regrets.

Finish what you start.

ELEVEN

GO FORWARD

My final game in the NFL came on January 3, 2010.
As described in the previous chapter, I was signed
by the Steelers late into the 2009 season and played
with them until the season finale, a game versus
the Dolphins in Miami. Even though we wouldn't
go to the playoffs, we ended the season on a high
note beating the Dolphins 30-24. Making the day
even better, I had two nice tackles on the kickoff
coverage team. Being a member of the Pittsburgh
Steelers, even for just those six games, had been
an honor. After the game I showered, dressed, and
headed out of the visiting locker room toward the
team buses parked outside the stadium. On my way
there however, I made a quick diversion back out
onto the field for one last look. It was a cool scene.

Nobody else was out there except the clean-up crew rummaging through the stands picking up litter and the groundskeepers manicuring the turf. I took a brief moment to reflect on my football life.

I first started playing football as a kid at age seven in a youth league in my hometown of Cincinnati, Ohio. I was now almost 30 years old and had just completed my eighth season in the NFL. It's amazing how fast it went. I thought about my NFL career. The ups and downs. The three times I got cut. The time I won the Super Bowl. All the injuries I had fought through. The good and bad plays I had made. Mostly I thought about all the great memories I had with my teammates during those eight seasons. In my heart I knew that my professional football career was over but I was satisfied and proud.

I finally walked onto the bus and as it was pulling away, my mind shifted to "what's next?" I had played football at some level for 23-straight years, the majority of my life. I couldn't even remember life before playing football. I certainly had other interests along the way, but my number one focus was always to reach the top as a football player and I didn't want the safety net of a backup plan. Creating a situation where failure was not an option had propelled me through all the dark times when a life in football didn't look like it was going to come true. But now it was time to actively get to work on what I wanted to do with the rest of my life. It was actually very exciting. The possibilities were limitless.

As the coming weeks and months would show however, turning new dreams into new realities was a very difficult thing to do. Playing football was something that always came natural and easy to me. The other careers I contemplated pursuing weren't falling into place at all. Making things even tougher, the structure of the NFL schedule was now gone. The days were long and aimless with no strict agenda to guide me.

I was rudderless. I got angry a lot. I often wasn't fun to be around. I sometimes didn't treat people very nicely. Trying to find a second act that was even remotely close to being as gratifying as playing football on an NFL field was looking to be fruitless. I missed the locker room. I missed the guidance of the great coaches I had been around. I missed being surrounded by amazingly talented people every day. To soften my new reality, I often spent my days traveling down memory lane. It was very easy to do and often encouraged by the people around me. No one can ever get enough of those NFL stories. I was trying to move on but couldn't.

It was my dad who finally snapped me out of it. He had been with me through it all and was a big reason I made it as far as I did. I was struggling and stagnant, but the guy who loved watching me play football wasn't going to let me reminisce my life away. I still remember what my dad said: "Rocky, the greatest contribution you're going to make to this world isn't going to be on a football field. This isn't it. Quit looking back and go FORWARD."

My dad encouraged me to spend every single second of my coming days in the present and not in the past. So, I filled my day with as many early morning coffee meetings, lunches, and phone calls with people as possible. Then I did the same thing the next day. Then the next. Anybody I could meet with, I did. Anyone out there who could give me an idea, inspire a thought, and give me some wisdom on what my next path might be I sought their advice.

One of the defining characteristics of a great NFL player, or any truly outstanding athlete, is the ability to have a "short memory." When they get beat, they have the ability to quickly flush it from their mind so they can perform well on the next play. A cornerback who gets burned for a touchdown must find a way to immediately gather his mind, drown out all the boos, retain his confidence, and go out there and shut his opponent down for the rest of the game. A quarterback who throws a crucial late interception must find a way to put that error aside and come out the very next series and lead the offense on a touchdown drive. The linebacker who gets trucked by a running back in front of an entire arena of fans, must find a way to shake off that embarrassment and come back the next play and make a stop.

Less talked about however is the fact that a player or team also must be able to move on from success. Soaking up the glory too long after an outstanding play or a great win can cause a player to lose focus and get complacent. The wide receiver who catches the winning touchdown can't allow that triumphant moment to go to his head and make him arrogant. The defensive end who has a four-sack performance cannot allow that heroic feat to make him so satisfied that he slacks off the next week. The team that has opened the season 9-0 can't allow themselves to relax, as defeat and embarrassment are only one game away.

One of the greatest lessons football teaches those who play it is that no matter what, in life you are only as good as your next play. This mindset is a characteristic that every player who goes on to have a career in the NFL, and not just a quick stop, must acquire. It is essential because in that high-stakes arena, with the world watching, there are going to be times you get beat and times you have success, no matter who you are. The only thing that matters is how you respond.

What I have found very interesting since I have retired though, is the number of former players who can't seem to move on from that special time in their lives where they were living the dream of playing in the NFL. I myself experienced it for a while after hanging it up. But for many guys, years after retirement, they continue to sit around and not do much with their lives. You see them frequently posting pictures of themselves in their uniform on social media and thinking back to that time they were on top of the world. Former players love to talk about a play they made or a game they won, ever eager to revisit the glory days. All the while doing nothing to move on and try to find something else that gives their life meaning. So many former players are stuck living in the past, it's no wonder we hear so many stories of post-career depression, bankruptcy, and ruin.

The fact that many former players are in this situation is bewildering because the key trait that made them great as an athlete was their ability to move on to the next play or the next challenge without looking back. They were able to have a short memory when they got beat. They were able to not let a successful game go to their head. Why are all these guys now stuck in the past?

I was fortunate to snap out of my retrospective funk and not squander away my post-football life for too long. I remember at one point thinking that having retired from football at age 30 meant that, God willing, I was going to have another 40 plus years on this planet. That's a helluva long time to live in the past. All those people I sought guidance from after retirement really helped. I was able to get refocused on the future instead of living in the past. I made it my mission to move on and find something to become passionate about other than just playing football. I wasn't always successful in my new ventures. I tried and failed many times. There were business ideas that ended poorly. But by exploring multiple avenues, I learned a lot about what I had passion for and what I did not. There were some successes along the way, like starting an athletic training business as well as becoming a local elected official. It took years but I finally found my current niche in the broadcasting world calling college football games and becoming a radio talk show host.

I think one of life's greatest challenges is finding a way to not set up residence in our past. Because we have so much invested in our life's work, it's common to find so much comfort in our past success that we want to stay in that place. By the same token, when we fail, we tend to rehash that moment in our brains incessantly, constantly thinking about what we should have done differently. Either way, both a past success and a past failure can tear you up if you allow it.

Having a past negative experience define our lives is an all-too-common problem. I recently had a discussion with a 30-year-old man who had been in and out of prison most of his adult life. The core culprit was substance addiction. He said something that I will never forget: "Rocky, no matter how hard I try, I can't rip the rear-view mirror off my life," he said. He was saying that he couldn't turn the page. His past was marred by bad choices, bad relationships, and depression so awful that he felt he couldn't move on. I pleaded with him to leave those poor decisions behind. I encouraged him to turn his back on those people who dragged him down and try to start anew. That is easier said than done. He kept dwelling on the past and not moving forward.

At the opposite extreme, the same trap of not moving forward can happen to the person who has experienced profound success. It's the sharp, young businessman who makes an early fortune only to squander it by not being driven to have repeat success. It's the cop who finds his name in the press for heroically saving a young child's life but doesn't show up the next day with that same desire to serve and protect. It's the lawyer who wins a big case and thinks that will carry her for the rest of her career. It's the researcher who gets complacent and stops looking for that next great discovery. These folks are the same as the athlete who spends so much time reminiscing about past glory that they look around and find that life has passed them by.

We all need to take a quick glimpse back at the past every once in a while. We need to relive the joy of a great moment in our lives and allow that feeling of accomplishment to give us confidence. We also need to, from time to time, recall a bad decision that we made and the valuable lesson we learned from it. We just can't look back too long. We can't stay there. No matter how good or how bad that decision, that moment, or that time period was, the past is something we now have zero control over.

Take a trip down memory lane once in a while but do not set up residence in the past. Boldly move forward. Strive for repeat success. Find another purpose that gives you joy. Discover a hidden talent that you never knew you had. Life is meant to be lived not remembered.

No matter how high or how low a particular moment was, you MUST go forward.

Rip off that rear view mirror. Go! Forward!

ACKNOWLEDGMENTS

I would like to thank my brilliant friend Mack Mariani for his guidance and suggestions on how to make this book the best it can be. You have helped me craft something that, in my opinion, is truly fantastic and I am beyond appreciative. I also want to thank my pals Pat Maloney and Paul Daugherty for their help and thoughtful advice in writing the book as well. To all the coaches, teammates, friends, and loved ones who have been there for me throughout my life, I am sincerely grateful.

ABOUT THE AUTHOR

Rocky Boiman is a college football analyst for ESPN and talk radio host on 700WLW in Cincinnati. He played football for the University of Notre Dame, serving as captain his senior year in 2001. He is also an eight-year veteran of the NFL having played for the Titans, Colts, Chiefs, and Steelers and winning a Super Bowl with the Colts in 2006. He now resides in his hometown of Cincinnati, Ohio, with his wife, Kelli, and their three sons Beau, Bronson, and Bryce.